31598
5/07

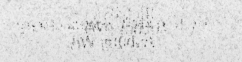

FLEEING TO FREEDOM ON THE UNDERGROUND RAILROAD

I'll go, or die in the attempt a trying. I'll walk as long as there's land, and if I come to the sea, I'll swim till I get drowned. I never expect you'll see me again; if they try to take me I'll fight till I die.

~John Holmes,
a runaway slave from Virginia,
speaking to another plantation slave before escaping, 1770

FLEEING TO FREEDOM ON THE UNDERGROUND RAILROAD

The Courageous Slaves, Agents, and Conductors

ELAINE LANDAU

TWENTY-FIRST CENTURY BOOKS · MINNEAPOLIS

For Klara Sweeney and Hailey Albers

A Word about Language
English word usage, spelling, grammar, and punctuation have changed over the centuries. We have preserved dialect and original spellings, as well as outdated terms such as *negro,* in the quotations included in this book.

Text copyright © 2006 by Elaine Landau

Twenty-First Century Books
A division of Lerner Publishing Group
241 First Avenue North
Minneapolis, Minnesota 55401 U.S.A.

Website address: www.lernerbooks.com

Library of Congress Cataloging-in-Publication Data

Landau, Elaine.
    Fleeing to freedom on the Underground Railroad : the courageous slaves, agents, and conductors / by Elaine Landau.
        p.   cm. — (People's history)
    Includes bibliographical references and index.
    ISBN-13: 978–0–8225–3490–7 (lib. bdg. : alk. paper)
    ISBN-10: 0–8225–3490–8 (lib. bdg. : alk. paper)
    1. Underground railroad—Juvenile literature. 2. Fugitive slaves—United States—History—19th century—Juvenile literature. 3. Antislavery movements—United States—History—19th century—Juvenile literature. 4. Abolitionists—United States—History—19th century—Juvenile literature. 5. Slavery—United States—History—Juvenile literature. I. Title. II. Series.
    E450.L3155   2006
    973.7'115—dc22   2005020358

Manufactured in the United States of America
1 2 3 4 5 6 – JR – 11 10 09 08 07 06

CONTENTS

[S]laves] are no more, in the sight of their masters, than the cotton they plant, or the horses they tend.
—Harriet Jacobs, a slave born in 1893

INTRODUCTION

From the 1500s to the mid-1800s, slavery was the economic and social grounding of a large part of agricultural America. It was a brutal life for the millions of African Americans who were forced to toil as slaves on southern plantations without pay and without legal rights. As a result, thousands of slaves fled to the northern United States and to Canada, where slavery was outlawed.

While slavery remained legal in parts of the United States, slave owners could do anything they wanted to try to capture runaways. Trained dogs, armed slave catchers, and death were among the many dangers runaway slaves faced. Yet they continued to run. The odds were against them, but some slaves felt they had no other real choice. Despite living in a country founded on the principles of liberty and justice, these individuals had been denied the most basic kinds of freedom.

Slaves were the property of their masters and had no control over their daily lives. They could be made to work long hours under the hot sun. They could be beaten and nearly starved to death if it suited their owners. Slaves were not permitted to marry without their master's consent, and even then there were no guarantees that a slave family would be allowed to stay together. At any time, a husband, wife, or child might be sold to another owner and the family separated forever. A slave's life was filled with uncertainty and humiliation. That was the reality of slavery—the undeniable truth that enslaved African Americans faced every day.

Facing page: *A slave family in the cotton fields on a plantation near Savannah, Georgia, in the early 1860s. Cotton picking was hard labor, but even children were expected to work in the fields.*

How many family ties have been broken by the cruel hand of slavery.
—James L. Smith, a former slave, in his 1881 autobiography

THE WAY IT WAS

In the seventeenth and eighteenth centuries, many colonists from England and other countries in Europe came to America seeking freedom. Some came for religious freedom, determined to worship as they wished. Others came for economic freedom—to be free to work for themselves rather than for a king or a landlord. They wanted to own their farms and houses and work for their money to the best of their abilities. Many colonists also wanted the political freedom to choose their own leaders and organize their own local governments.

In fact, in the late eighteenth century, American colonists went to war against Great Britain to secure these freedoms. After winning the American Revolution (1775–1783), colonial leaders formed the

United States of America. But the United States was not a free nation for everyone. Hundreds of thousands of African Americans lived in slavery.

In many states in the northern part of the country, slavery was unpopular. Some northern states began passing laws against it. For example, as early as the 1780s, Pennsylvania's state legislature took a step in that direction with the Gradual Abolition of Slavery Act. This law contained a number of provisions designed to end slavery in Pennsylvania. And in 1808, the U.S. Congress banned the continued importation of slaves—the practice of capturing Africans in their own countries and shipping them to the United States.

However, while slavery decreased in the North, the number of slaves in southern states greatly increased. Slavery, in fact, formed the basis of

Right: *Africans were captured in their homelands and brought on ships to North American colonies as early as the 1600s. The journey was long and torturous, and those who survived the trip were sold into slavery.* Facing page: *A slave father is sold away from his family.*

the southern economy. Southern slavery was driven by the rise of the plantation system, in which crops such as tobacco, sugar, rice, hemp, cotton, and indigo were grown on large farming estates. Plantation owners poured their money into the land, buildings, livestock, and machinery necessary for these huge ongoing operations. They could not afford to also pay fair wages to the many workers needed to plant and harvest the crops. Servants were also needed for domestic work in the plantation houses, such as cooking, cleaning, and taking care of children—all without the aid of modern conveniences. Without the free labor of slavery, the plantations would not have been profitable.

In the mid-1800s, an overseer (a work supervisor) weighs bushels of cotton handpicked by slaves. The backbreaking work that slaves did on cotton and other plantations provided free labor and allowed plantation owners to make huge profits.

Many slave owners treated their slaves with unfathomable cruelty. Masters could whip their slaves for any offense, large or small.

After importing slaves into the United States became illegal, southern states began a local slave trade to ensure that plantations and farms were well stocked with field-workers and house servants. American-born descendants of African slaves—men, women, and children—were sold at auctions from Virginia to the Carolinas to Georgia, Alabama, and parts of Texas. By the mid-ninteenth century, census figures indicated that almost four million African American slaves lived in the United States.

Slavery allowed some plantation owners to acquire great wealth. But the human misery that supported the system was staggering. Slaveholders became the guardians of a cruel system in which slaves were often treated worse than farm animals. Slave owners regarded

Slaves had to demonstrate humiliating obedience to whites, as shown in this illustration of colonial America from Harper's Weekly.

their slaves as property, rather than people. Supporters of slavery tried to convince themselves and others of the righteousness of the system by arguing that the white race was superior. They came up with a broad array of historical and biblical reasons why African Americans were better off as slaves. And as slaves, African Americans owed everything, even their lives, to their owners. As a southern judge once decreed, "The power of the master must be absolute."

A Slave's Life

To maintain absolute authority, slaveholders aimed to break all emotional ties among slave families. Slaveholders often broke up slave families, selling family members to various buyers. Husbands and wives purchased by different owners might never see one another again. Children were often separated from their parents and their siblings at a very young age. Robert Glen, a former slave, was eighty-seven years old when he was interviewed for a U.S. government oral history project that aimed to document slave life after the institution came to an end. Glen described what it was like for him to be sold as a young boy:

> *I belonged to a man named Bob Hall. . . . He died when I was eight years old and I was put on the [auction] block and sold. . . . I saw my brother and sister sold on this same plantation. . . . They sold me away from my mother and father. . . . I was not allowed to tell my mother and father good bye.*

Some slaves managed to buy or win their freedom. The southern slave trade also victimized these free African Americans. Some were kidnapped by unscrupulous whites and illegally sold back into bondage.

Often young children were prime targets for these kidnapping schemes. Children could be easily stolen while their parents were working or when the children were playing outdoors on their own. It happened to two very young African American boys from New Jersey, brothers named Peter and Levin Still. Peter and Levin's mother was a free woman, so Peter and Levin were also free.

One day, the boys were playing alone by the road near their home. A white man driving a carriage stopped to inquire where their mother was. The boys told the man that their mother was at church. The friendly stranger offered to take them to her. Thinking it would be fun to surprise their mother, the boys eagerly agreed.

After riding in the carriage for a while, Peter, Levin, and the man boarded a boat. Peter and Levin were becoming tired and anxious about being away from home for so long. But the man assured them that they would soon see their mother. Encouraging the boys to trust him, the man spoke softly and gave them sweets. The boys didn't realize that they had been kidnapped and that the man was taking them to the slave state of Kentucky. Peter Still's biographer, Kate E. R. Pickard, tells what happened once they arrived in Kentucky:

> [The kidnapper] took them to a plain brick house where dwelt one John Fisher, a mason by trade, and proprietor of a large brick yard. After some conversation between the gentlemen, which of course the children did not understand, [the children] were taken out to the kitchen, and presented to Aunt Betty, the cook.
>
> "There, my boys," said [the kidnapper] "there is your mother—we've found her at last." "No! No!" they shrieked, "That's not our mother! O, please sir! Take us back!" With tears and cries they . . . begged him not to leave them there. This scene was soon ended by John Fisher himself, who, with a hearty blow on each cheek bade them "hush!" "You belong to me now, you little rascals, and I'll have no more of this."

The boys' kidnapper had sold them to John Fisher, and they were now Fisher's slaves. Peter Still soon learned that being a slave meant that you had no control over your life. Many slaves were forced to work long hours under brutal conditions. Though just a child, Peter saw that a slave could be subjected to torturous punishments at the whim of a master or an overseer.

When Peter was nine years old, Fisher put him to work in the brickyard in a job called an off-bearer. Peter and another boy had to prepare three thousand bricks for the kiln each day. If one of the pair was unable to work for any reason, the other was expected to "off-bear," or do all the work himself.

Those who failed to live up to the task were punished on the spot. Peter recalled one common method of punishment:

> [The overseer's] favorite mode of chastisement [punishment] was called "standing in the wheelbarrow." The offender was placed

with a foot on each side of the wheel, and compelled to reach over and grasp a handle in each hand; and then the youngest boys—the "off-bearers"—were compelled to whip him with cowhides. If [the one being whipped] would lie still and take twenty-four lashes without attempting to rise, that was deemed sufficient proof of his humility. But if he made an effort to change his position before that number was inflicted . . . [the person] who counted off the strokes, commenced again at "one," and caused the twenty-four to be repeated.

In other situations, slaves were whipped or beaten even more severely. Wanted posters describing runaway slaves often contained phrases such as "large scar on hip," "no marks except those on back," "much scarred with the whip," and "will no doubt show the marks of a recent whipping."

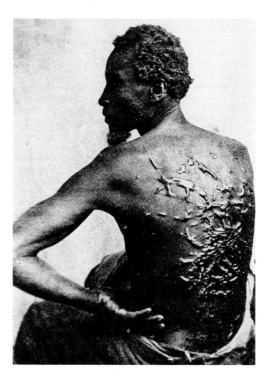

This slave's back is severely scarred from being whipped.

Slave quarters on many southern plantations provided only the most basic necessities. This photo was taken in South Carolina in 1862.

The Worst Conditions

In addition to enduring harsh punishments, slaves lived in terrible conditions. Crowded into poorly built shacks, they were exposed to both freezing cold and extreme heat. They were often given barely enough to eat and never allowed a full night's sleep.

On many plantations, slaves worked from sun up to sunset with little time to rest. In cases where overseers were paid bonuses for increasing production, slaves were worked particularly hard. In his autobiography, Solomon Northup, a free African American who was kidnapped and sold into bondage, described the workday on a Louisiana plantation:

The hands [slaves] are required to be in the cotton field as soon as it is light in the morning, and, with the exception of ten or fifteen minutes, which is given them at noon to swallow their allowance of cold bacon, they are not permitted to be a moment idle until it is too dark to see, and when the moon is full, they often times labor till the middle of the night.

Northup reported that the slaves had more duties after leaving the fields. "Each one must attend to his respective chores," he continued. "One feeds the mules, another the swine—another cuts the wood, and so forth; besides the packing [of cotton] is all done by candle light. Finally, at a late hour, they reach the [slave] quarters, sleepy and overcome with the long day's toil."

Slaves across the South endured similar conditions. Former slave Peter Randolph described the clothing given to slaves on the plantation where he lived. In *Sketches of Slave Life: Or, Illustrations of the "Peculiar Institution,"* Randolph noted that slaves were given one pair of shoes for the entire year. If the shoes wore out within a couple of months, the slave had to go barefoot for the rest of the year, even through winter. Likewise, Randolph explained, slaves got one suit of cheap clothes and one hat for the year.

On some plantations, slaves were allowed to grow vegetable gardens to supplement the scant food they were given. And sometimes rations were increased during planting and harvesting times, as plantation owners wanted their workers to have enough strength to do the job. But for the most part, slaves usually remained hungry much of the time. Randolph described the slaves' food rations:

Every Saturday night, [male slaves] receive two pounds of bacon, and one peck and a half of corn meal, to last the men through the week. . . . When this is gone, they can have no more till the end of the week. This is very little food for the slaves. They have to beg when they can; when they cannot, they must suffer. They are not allowed to go off the plantation; if they do, and are caught, they are whipped very severely, and what they begged for is taken from them.

In the Woods and Swamps

Beaten, overworked, and starving, some slaves tried to escape. Some sprinted away from their work gang when the overseer's head was turned. Others crept off silently during the night. Many of the runaways first hid out in nearby woods and swamps. Some would stay in these hiding places, while others traveled on to small islands or up into nearby mountains. The runaways all survived by living off the land, hunting small animals and gathering plants for food. They lived in caves or crudely made huts. Sometimes they managed to sneak back to the plantation to get their wives and children.

A few formed communities of runaway slaves who did their best to stay hidden from whites. Other fleeing slaves, ever alert to the possibility of capture, preferred to live alone and stay on the move. In his narrative, *A Slave's Story,* former slave Ralph Roberts described what it was like to remain on the run:

> *In one instance, I knew two men to live more than a year in a cave, in a large wood, about a mile from their master's house. The [animals] on the adjacent farms supplied them with meat, and [other scraps were] easily gotten from their fellow-slaves— for, in almost every such case, regular communication is kept up between the fugitive and his class [other slaves]. . . . This is done with all possible precaution. Least some white person detects them. But they never fear a betrayal from one of their own race; nor will the hope of reward or the fear of punishment generally extort any information that might lead to the capture of the fugitive.*

A group of escaped slaves hides out in the swamps of Louisiana. Escaped slaves helped each other in any way they could. They faced incredible dangers, but to many slaves, the risk of capture was worth taking if it meant gaining freedom.

The Underground Railroad

With the passage of time, new safe havens opened to runaways. People in the North grew increasingly opposed to slavery, and more northern states banned it. The abolition of slavery in the North heightened tensions between the North and South. Some northerners began to campaign for the abolition of slavery throughout the entire country. But southern slave owners felt that this idea threatened their way of life, so they vehemently opposed it.

Slave owners tried to keep their slaves ignorant of the growing number of free states. But before long, stories of successful slave escapes to the North spread from plantation to plantation. Slaves began to hear about northerners who believed that all human beings, regardless of color, were entitled to be free.

These northerners came from all walks of life, but they had one thing in common. They were willing to take risks to help others find freedom. At times they sheltered exhausted runaways from slave catchers who pursued them with rifles and dogs. They fed and hid the fugitive slaves before directing them to other places of refuge along the route to freedom.

These loose and often informal arrangements were the start of an assisted escape network for slaves known as the Underground Railroad. The Underground Railroad was essential in helping runaway slaves reach the free states that bordered the South, such as Ohio, Pennsylvania, Indiana, and Illinois. The Underground Railroad was extremely

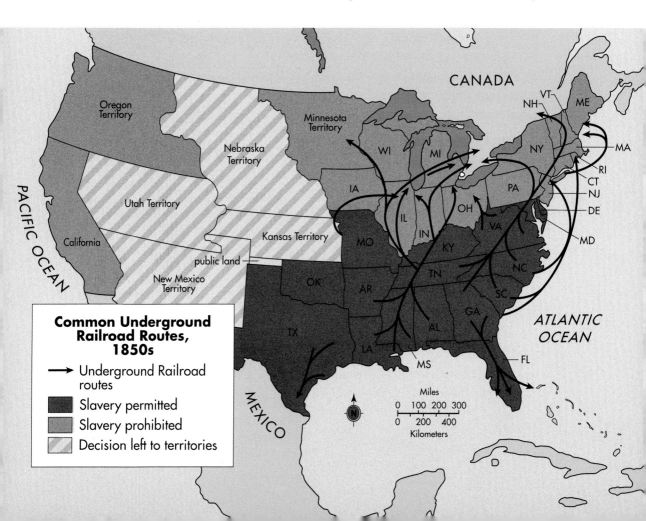

Common Underground Railroad Routes, 1850s

→ Underground Railroad routes
■ Slavery permitted
■ Slavery prohibited
▨ Decision left to territories

active in these border states, but its work did not stop there. Dedicated volunteers also helped the runaways settle in free areas farther north, including Canada, and find housing and work there.

To a large extent, the Underground Railroad was a secret system. It never became a well-organized national society with meetings and officials. Instead, it was simply made up of individuals who were against slavery and could do something to help escaping slaves. Underground Railroad workers were white and African American, old and young. Certain religious groups, such as the Quakers, who had strong beliefs against slavery, also supported the Railroad.

In reality, the Underground Railroad was neither underground nor a railroad. No one is certain how it got its name. However, in his book, *The Underground Railroad from Slavery to Freedom,* history professor Wilbur H. Siebert considers a frequently told story about how it might have happened.

In 1831, Siebert recounts, a fugitive slave named Tice Davids was headed for Ohio with his master, a Kentuckian, in close pursuit. As Davids reached the Ohio River, he realized that his master was so close that he (Davids) had no choice but to jump in the river and swim across. The slave master was forced to find a boat, but he kept Davids in his sights and saw him crawl up on the opposite shore. But when the master finally reached the shore, there was no trace of Davids anywhere. After a long search, the slave master went into the town of Ripley, Ohio, complaining that his runaway slave must have escaped on an underground road. Supposedly, the term *underground road* later became "underground railroad" and was used to describe secret escape routes for slaves.

Regardless of how it got its name, the Underground Railroad in time became increasingly widespread and effective. Some estimates suggest that between the American Revolution and the Civil War (1861–1865), as many as one hundred thousand slaves took this path to freedom.

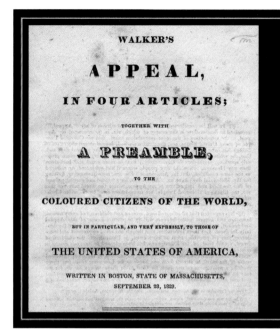

WALKER'S

APPEAL,

IN FOUR ARTICLES;

TOGETHER WITH

A PREAMBLE,

TO THE

COLOURED CITIZENS OF THE WORLD,

BUT IN PARTICULAR, AND VERY EXPRESSLY, TO THOSE OF

THE UNITED STATES OF AMERICA,

WRITTEN IN BOSTON, STATE OF MASSACHUSETTS,
SEPTEMBER 28, 1829.

Somebody must die in this cause. I may be doomed . . . , but it is not in me to falter.
—David Walker, African American abolitionist, 1830

THE ABOLITIONIST MOVEMENT

Though successful slave escapes had occurred since colonial times, the Underground Railroad became increasingly active between 1830 and 1860. This may have been at least partly due to an important growing social movement known as the abolitionist cause. Those supporting the abolition of slavery in the United States hoped to expose the inhumanity and injustice of a system that bought, sold, and brutalized people solely on the basis of skin color. The abolitionists wanted people to see slavery as a moral issue rather than as an economic choice.

Hoping to outlaw slavery throughout the United States, the abolitionists formed organizations to make their voices heard. Many of these societies started out as small local groups, but in 1833 the American Anti-Slavery Society was founded. This national organization served as a broad central base from which abolitionists could coordinate their programs. Some programs were political and involved distributing pamphlets and organizing lectures and rallies to sway public sentiment against slavery. Other programs were directly involved in assisting escaped slaves.

During its first few years, the American Anti-Slavery Society had about 400 chapters, mostly in the North. But by the late 1830s, the organization had grown to 1,350 chapters with a membership of more than 250,000 people.

Right: *An 1833 publication advertises a convention of the American Anti-Slavery Society. It outlines the goals of the group, and at the bottom, it lists the delegates from ten states who attended the convention.* Facing page: *The first page from African American abolitionist David Walker's* Appeal, *published in 1830.*

The growth of the movement had a tremendous impact on the scope and effectiveness of the Underground Railroad. Many members of abolitionist organizations became active participants in the Underground Railroad's workings. But even abolitionists who didn't work directly for the Railroad wholly supported it. They openly applauded its activities and helped it financially.

To some degree, the Underground Railroad functioned as the action arm of the abolitionist movement. Many of those with the Underground Railroad never gave a speech or took part in a protest rally. But by hiding escaped slaves in their homes or guiding them along the path to freedom, they brought the abolitionist sentiment to life. Some scholars feel that the Underground Railroad would not have been as widespread or accepted if the abolitionist press had not made northerners more aware of the cruelty and unfairness of slavery. Conversely, the abolitionist cause might have largely remained a movement of words rather than action without the Underground Railroad.

The *Liberator*

Among the leaders of the American Anti-Slavery Society was an outspoken abolitionist from Massachusetts named William Lloyd Garrison. Garrison became active in the abolitionist movement when he was just twenty-five. He soon became well known for his fiery abolitionist newspaper, the *Liberator,* published in Boston, Massachusetts. Garrison set forth the publication's purpose and tone in its first issue with a strong call for change. Stressing that he wanted both freedom and citizenship for enslaved African Americans, Garrison wrote the following stinging editorial in 1831:

> On this subject [slavery], I do not wish to think, or speak, or write, with moderation. No! No! Tell a man whose house is on fire to give a moderate alarm; tell him to moderately rescue his wife from the hands of a ravisher; tell the mother to gradually

Abolitionist William Lloyd Garrison published the antislavery newspaper the **Liberator.**

extricate her babe from the fire into which it has fallen; — but urge me not to use moderation in a cause like the present. I am in earnest—I will not equivocate—I will not excuse—I will not retreat a single inch—AND I WILL BE HEARD.

The *Liberator* drew a mixed readership of antislavery northerners and nervous southern slaveholders who bought the paper to keep abreast of abolitionist activities and sentiment. The *Liberator* also served as a vital forum for those associated with the Underground Railroad. Railroad workers sent stories and letters to the paper describing slavery's evils and the hardships escaped slaves endured. The *Liberator* also frequently listed abolitionist meetings and events at which fugitive slaves who had reached the North spoke of their dangerous journeys to freedom.

For example, Garrison published the story of William and Ellen Craft. The Crafts were a slave couple. Ellen was twenty-two years old, and William was twenty-four. They used a clever disguise to escape the South with the help of the Underground Railroad. Their tale was described in a letter from an abolitionist that appeared in the *Liberator.*

> *DEAR FRIEND GARRISON:*
> *One of the most interesting cases of the escape of fugitives from American slavery . . . [is that of] William and Ellen Craft, a man and wife, [who] lived with different masters in the State of Georgia. Ellen is so near white, that she can pass without suspicion for a white woman. Her husband is much darker. He is a mechanic, and by working nights and Sundays [which his master allowed him to do] . . . he laid up money enough to bring himself and his wife out of slavery. . . . [To disguise herself] Ellen dressed in man's clothing, and passed as the master while her*

Ellen Craft disguised herself as a white master in order to escape with her husband to freedom in the North. This illustration showing her dressed as a man was published in the British newspaper the London Illustrated News *in 1851.*

husband [posed as her slave/servant]. . . . In this way they traveled from Georgia to Philadelphia. They are now out of the reach of the bloodhounds of the South. On their journey, they put up [stayed] at the best hotels where they stopped. Neither of them can read or write. And Ellen, knowing that she would be called upon to write her name at the hotels [in order to register] . . . tied her right hand up as though it was lame [injured]. . . . They arrived in Philadelphia, in four days from the time they started. Their history, especially that of their escape, is replete with interest. They will be at the meeting of the Massachusetts Anti-Slavery Society, in Boston, in the latter part of the month.

Yours, truly,
WM. W. Brown

African American Abolitionists

Many of the most active abolitionists were free African Americans. One of the earliest and perhaps the most outspoken African American abolitionists was David Walker. Though his father had been a slave, Walker was born to a free African American woman, so he was free as well. Walker owned and operated a used clothing business near Boston Harbor in Massachusetts. Walker published a pamphlet known as the *Appeal,* in which he challenged the hypocrisy of a supposedly free country that still allowed slavery. Citing the Declaration of Independence, Walker wrote:

Compare your own language. . . , extracted from your Declaration of Independence, with your cruelties and murders inflicted by your cruel and unmerciful fathers and yourselves on our fathers and on us—men who have never given your fathers or you the least provocation!!!!!!

A pro-slavery mob destroys an office and printing press where abolitionist material had been published. Abolitionists did not only have to worry about destruction of property; their personal safety was at stake as well.

In his *Appeal,* Walker urged slaves to rebel against their masters. Walker sewed copies of the document into the linings of the clothing he sold to African American sailors. When their ships docked in the South, the sailors secretly passed the copies to slaves and other southerners sympathetic to the abolitionist cause. Garrison also published Walker's *Appeal* in the *Liberator.*

Walker's writings shook slave owners to the core. They felt that it encouraged slaves to run away as well as rebel. Some slave owners offered a ten-thousand-dollar reward to anyone who could capture Walker and bring him to them in the South, where he would face lynching.

Walker's supporters, including those working with the Underground Railroad, urged him to go into hiding. They promised to help him get safely to Canada, but Walker refused to allow the slave owners to run him out of the country. He stood his ground and was never kidnapped and taken south.

Another African American abolitionist was a free man named David Ruggles. Ruggles was born in Connecticut and later moved to New York City to work as a grocer. Ruggles published a number of antislavery pamphlets and articles, but he became especially well known for his work on the New York Committee of Vigilance. Vigilance committees helped escaped slaves adjust to life in the free North. They became essential to the effective operation of the Underground Railroad system.

Once runaway slaves arrived safely in the North, vigilance committees helped the fugitives establish themselves as free individuals. Committee members taught the fugitives how to adopt a new identity, find suitable lodgings, and avoid slave catchers. The runaways needed work to support themselves, but they had to be careful in seeking jobs. Vigilance committees advertised in abolitionist newspapers to find employers sympathetic to runaway slaves. Committee members also provided the former slaves with letters of introduction to prospective employers.

Relocating large numbers of fugitive slaves could be costly, and runaways usually left their plantations penniless. They needed money for food, clothing, housing, and travel as soon as they arrived in the North. Sometimes the various abolitionist organizations helped out. The vigilance committees also often held special rallies as fund-raisers. The money they raised was vital to this phase of the Underground Railroad's work.

Ruggles sometimes worked around the clock to find employment and lodging for former slaves. He stood out for his energy and talent in helping runaways. Among the hundreds of escaped slaves Ruggles helped was Frederick Douglass. When Douglass arrived in the North, Ruggles took him in for a time. Once Douglass was ready to begin a new life for himself in the town of New Bedford, Massachusetts, Ruggles provided him with money and a letter of introduction.

Frederick Douglass, a former slave, is pictured here (at the table, far right) *attending an antislavery convention in 1845.*

In turn, Douglass became an Underground Railroad worker, helping escaped slaves as he had been helped. Frederick Douglass later described his ties to the Underground Railroad. He noted, "My connection with the Underground Railroad began long before I left the South, and was continued, whether I lived in New Bedford, Lynn [Massachusetts], or Rochester, N.Y. In the latter place, I had as many as eleven fugitives under my roof at one time."

Eventually Douglass became one of the best-known and most inspiring voices for the abolitionist cause. He was a tall, impressive man, and when he lectured at abolitionist meetings, his powerful words and voice moved the audiences. Frederick Douglass's writings were also extremely influential. He began an African American newspaper called the *North Star.* The paper's name came from a common term on the Underground Railroad. Fugitive slaves on the run were told to follow the North Star, a particularly bright star high in the sky, used in navigation at that time.

In countless instances, African Americans proved crucial to the success of the abolitionist cause and of the Underground Railroad. In some cases, runaways refused help from whites they did not know for fear of being tricked. They felt safe enough to continue only after seeing African American Railroad conductors. On one well-used Underground Railroad route through Ohio, more than one hundred free African Americans conducted fugitive slaves to freedom. In Saint Louis, Missouri, free African Americans helped transport runaways to Chicago, Illinois, and other northern cities.

The African American abolitionists and Underground Railroad volunteers were risking their lives. Some were runaway slaves themselves, but they traveled back to the South to bring other slaves out. Some went back to get family members out, but many went back to help free slaves they did not even know. The advantage was that the former slaves knew the territory well and had the trust of runaways. Their commitment to the abolitionist cause and to the Underground Railroad was clear.

One hundred dollar reward for my negro Glasgow and Kate, his wife.
—an 1837 newspaper advertisement

ESCAPE!

Slave owners frequently posted rewards for their escaped slaves in newspapers throughout the South. Runaway slaves resulted in lost work, and moreover, slaves were costly to replace. As a result, slave owners were willing to pay reward money or hire slave catchers for the return of fugitives. Some slave owners even pursued their fugitives themselves. The success of the Underground Railroad in assisting escapes and foiling slave catchers was a complex challenge for slave owners. It took away slave owners' "property" permanently and, at the same time, suggested to other slaves that running away was an option for them too.

Because slave owners wanted to end the Underground Railroad's operations, the Railroad operated in strict secrecy. Slave owners could not effectively strike back at an enemy they could not find.

Agents and conductors—as Underground Railroad volunteers were called—had to be creative and flexible. They had to learn to expect the unexpected to avoid slave owners and slave catchers. The lives of thousands of slaves were ultimately at stake, with little room for error.

Shipped in a Box

Some escapes were truly remarkable. For example, Henry "Box" Brown, a slave from Virginia, escaped by shipping himself to the North. While a slave, Brown had been hired out by his master to work in a tobacco factory in Richmond, Virginia. Brown's master allowed him to keep a small part of his factory wages. During that time, Brown married a slave owned by another master. His wife's master promised never to sell Brown's wife as long as Brown paid him part of his small earnings.

Brown made his payments, but his wife's owner broke his promise. The owner sold Brown's wife and the couple's three children to a new master from another southern state. Brown could do nothing to stop the sale of his family. At that point, Brown decided that he could no longer remain a slave. With no emotional bonds to keep him in the South anymore, he grew determined to run away.

Before long, Brown came up with an unusual and dangerous escape plan. He bought a box three feet long, two feet wide, and two and one-half feet deep. He made arrangements to have the box sent from Richmond, Virginia, to Philadelphia, Pennsylvania, to the home of some Underground Railroad workers. Then Brown crawled inside the box, and friends nailed the lid shut.

The trip took twenty-seven hours. Mr. M. McRoy received the box in Philadelphia and helped uncrate Brown. Inspired by Brown's courage and strength, McRoy wrote a letter of introduction for Brown, describing how his daring escape had worked.

Here is the man [Henry Brown] who has been the hero of one of the most extraordinary achievements I ever heard of—he came to me on

Saturday Morning last, in a box . . . marked "THIS SIDE UP. . . . " It was a regular old store box . . . grooved at the joints and braced at the ends, leaving but the very slightest crevice to admit the air. Nothing saved him from suffocation but the free use of water—a quantity of which he took in [the box] with him . . . and with which he bathed his face—and the constant fanning of himself with a hat. . . . The "THIS SIDE" on the box was not [always] regarded [paid attention to], and he was twice put with his head downward . . . the first time he succeeded in shifting his position; but the second time was on board a steam boat, where people were sitting and standing about the box, and where any motions inside would have been overheard and have led to discovery; he was therefore obligated to keep his position for twenty miles. This nearly killed him. . . . He will tell you the whole story. Please send him on to Mr. McGleveland, Boston, with this letter.

Henry "Box" Brown arrived, shaken but unharmed, in Philadelphia in 1849. In a clever escape, Brown mailed himself to freedom. In this portrayal, the artist depicts Frederick Douglass (second from left) *helping to open the box.*

Escape Routes

For a time, many slaves from Georgia went south to the Spanish-controlled Florida Territory (modern-day Florida). Some of these fugitives lived among the area's Seminole Indians, while others found acceptance in some of the growing Spanish towns.

For slaves in Mississippi, Alabama, and Louisiana, however, the closest escape route was to Mexico. Mexico at that time included land in what is the modern-day southwestern United States. Slave owners pressured the U.S. Congress to try to work out a treaty with Mexico in 1827 that would guarantee that slaves who had fled there the would be returned to their masters. However, Mexico refused to agree to such a treaty and instead amended its constitution to grant freedom as well as equal rights to these African Americans.

However, once the United States acquired Florida and the Mexican territories in the Southwest, slaveholders were in a better position. Then, for even slaves in the Deep South, freedom lay in only one direction: north.

Many fugitive slaves headed to northern states where slavery had been banned. However, they were not always entirely safe in the North. There was always the danger of being captured and returned by slave catchers. So many ran even farther north to Canada.

The Underground Railroad's Organization

Answering the needs of escaping slaves, the Underground Railroad system grew quite extensive. It stretched from Kentucky and Virginia across Ohio, and from Maryland through Pennsylvania, New York, and New England to Canada. Underground Railroad lines and stations filled Indiana, Illinois, Iowa, and all the states east of the Mississippi River that existed at the time.

The terms used to describe the workings of the Underground Railroad were similar to those used on an actual railroad. On an actual railroad, stations or depots are regular stops along train routes. They often have buildings where passengers can rest and wait for the next train. On the Underground Railroad, depots or stations were safe houses, people's homes where runaway slaves hid and rested during the daylight hours after traveling all night. Stations were usually between ten and twenty miles apart along the Underground Railroad routes.

On an actual railroad, agents sell train tickets and assist passengers at stations or depots. Conductors travel on the trains to assist passengers along the way. Underground Railroad conductors were volunteers who traveled along the routes to help slaves escape and reach the nearest station. Underground Railroad agents (sometimes called superintendents) offered their homes as Railroad stations and took care of arriving runaways. If that was not possible, agents secured

In one of the stops along the Underground Railroad, runaway slaves are helped to a hiding place. Brave conductors risked fines and even jail to help the fugitives.

Runaway slaves are stopped by slave catchers. If captured, runaways were returned to the South and to slavery, where they usually faced harsh punishments and sometimes death for their actions.

other hideouts, such as abandoned barns or caves. When not working directly with runaways, agents helped design escape routes, approved changes to escape plans, and collected funds to benefit the fugitives.

A Close Call

Agents always had to be on the lookout for slave catchers or fugitive slaves' owners in the area. If a slave catcher or owner suspected that an agent was lying about hiding runaways, the catcher or owner might pretend to leave the area. But he would actually remain nearby, keeping a close watch on the agent's house and movements.

Agents and runaways endured some very close calls. Sidney Speed of Crawfordsville, Indiana, was the son of Underground Railroad conductor John Speed. He described one such incident at his father's house:

> *A mulatto [mixed race] girl about eighteen or twenty years old, very good looking and with some education . . . reached our home. The . . . [slave] catchers became so watchful that she could*

not be moved for several days. In fact, some of them were nearly
always at the house either on some pretended business or making
social visits. I do not think that the house was searched, or they
would surely have found her, as during all this time she
remained in the garret over the old log kitchen, where the
fugitives were usually kept when there was danger. Her owner, a
man from New Orleans [Louisiana], had just bought her in
Louisville [Kentucky], and he had traced her surely to this place;
she had not struck the Underground [Railroad] before, but had
made her way alone this far, and as they [her owner and those
with him] got no trace of her beyond here they returned and
doubled the watches on . . . my father. But at length a day came,
or a night rather, when she was safely led out through the garden
to the house of a colored man [with the Underground Railroad]
named Patterson.

Though the young woman safely left John Speed's house, Underground Railroad conductors still faced the challenge of getting her to Canada. They decided that the light-skinned runaway would make the journey disguised as a white woman. One of Patterson's daughters and the white baby of an abolitionist would accompany the young woman part of the way. The idea was for people to think that the runaway was a well-to-do white woman traveling with her baby and her maid.

All three were to take the train to Detroit, Michigan, and then separate. The disguised fugitive would board a ferry to cross the Detroit River into Canada while the Patterson girl and the baby took the train back to Indiana. Sidney Speed described a frightening surprise as the escape proceeded:

[The runaway slave] was rigged out in as fine a costume of silk
and ribbons as it was possible to procure at that time, and was
furnished with a white baby borrowed for the occasion, and

accompanied by one of the Patterson girls as servant and nurse. Thus disguised, the lady boarded the train at the station. But what must have been her feelings to find her master already in the same [train] car; he was setting out to watch for her at the end of the line.

The fugitive slave had to ride in the same train car as her owner, hoping he would not recognize her. But the terrifying trip ended well:

She kept her courage, and when they reached Detroit she went aboard the ferry-boat for Canada . . . and as the gang-plank was being raised, the young slave-woman on the boat removed her veil that she might bid her master good bye. [It was safe to do so as the ferry had already pulled out and would not stop again until it docked in Canada.] The master's display of anger as he gazed at the departing boat was as real as the situation was gratifying to his former slave and amusing to the bystanders.

I'll go, or die in the attempt a trying. I'll walk as long as there's land.
—John Holms, a runaway slave from Virginia, 1770

ON FREEDOM'S PATH

Successfully escaping to the North was never easy. The Underground Railroad did not have enough conductors to guide every escaping slave to the nearest station. Some slaves had to make their way on their own. For many, this was challenge enough. Slaves born on plantations may have never been more than a few miles from home. When they ran away, they faced the problem of navigating unfamiliar areas in the dark—and often while being pursued by dogs or slaveholders. Underground Railroad conductors had to provide some advice and rules for helping these slaves escape safely.

Most runaways began their journeys to freedom on foot. They did not have maps or compasses, and they could not stop and ask directions. So to make sure the slaves were headed the right way,

Underground Railroad workers secretly spread the word among plantation slaves to look in the night sky for the North Star. This is the brightest star near the Big Dipper constellation. If a slave decided to run away, he or she could follow the North Star to freedom. Slaves passed on the advice among themselves.

As one escaped slave wrote in a letter to an abolitionist newspaper: "The North Star was, in many instances, the only friend that the weary and footsore fugitive found on his pilgrimage to his new home among strangers."

On cloudy nights when they could not see the North Star, runaways checked the trees in wooded areas. Moss usually grows on the north side of tree trunks, providing a clue to help the slaves to stay

Right: *Most slaves escaped on foot, carrying what little they could on their backs. They often depended on the kindness of others to help them make their way north to freedom. Facing page: A slave family makes an escape on horseback in this 1862 painting by artist Eastman Johnson entitled* A Ride for Liberty—The Fugitive Slaves. *Eastman based his painting on an incident he personally witnessed.*

A slave tries to stay a step ahead of slave catchers and their dog.

on course. Slaves were also encouraged to look for certain local land-marks that they knew lay north of their masters' plantations. Yet even with these guides, runaways easily became confused and could actually travel some distance in the wrong direction. In these cases, the fugitive slaves had to discover their error before someone discovered them.

After traveling all night, fugitive slaves usually spent their days in hiding. Daniel Fisher, a Virginia slave who escaped with another slave, later detailed their experience:

We kept on our way on foot, hiding by day and walking by night. We were without knowledge of the country, and with nothing to guide us other than the north star, which was oftentimes obscured by clouds [on those nights], we would unwittingly retrace our steps and find ourselves back at the starting point. Finally after days of tedious walking. . . , fearing to ask for food and getting but little from the slaves we met, we [neared our destination].

Arriving at an Underground Railroad Station

After arriving at Underground Railroad depots or stations, runaways would wait until nightfall. Under the cover of dark, they would approach a depot door or window, tapping to signal that they were outside. In some parts of the country, Underground Railroad agents worked out other signals as well. At times, fugitive slaves were told to make a certain bird or animal call to let the agents know that they were there.

In some cases, Underground Railroad agents knew in advance that runaway slaves were on the way. Agents from earlier stops sent notes urging people down the line to be on the lookout for fugitives needing help. Usually, these messages were cleverly worded to disguise their meaning in case the notes fell into the wrong hands. For example, the following notes were written by Underground Railroad agents to other agents:

Mr. C. B. C.

Dear Sir: By tomorrow evening's mail, you will receive two volumes of the "Irrepressible Conflict" bound in black. After perusal, please forward, and oblige,

Yours truly,
G. W. W.

Dear Grinnell:

Uncle Tom says that if the roads are not too bad, you can look for those fleeces of wool by to-morrow. Send them on to test the market and price, no back charges.

Yours,
Hub

In both these notes, everyday objects—volumes of books or wool fleeces—are code for arriving slaves. Instructions to "please forward" or to send on to the market indicated that the agent receiving the note should send the slaves to the next Railroad station.

While at an Underground Railroad station, fugitive slaves were given a good meal, a change of clothes, and a chance to talk about their experiences. The families living at the stations were used to having runaways as their guests and always had hiding places ready for the fugitives. This was crucial to everyone's safety. At any time, a well-armed slave owner or slave catcher could arrive on the premises and demand to search the house.

To prepare for this, secret hiding places were often built into the Underground Railroad agent's home or barn. These included trap-doors hidden under rugs that led to a dug out space beneath the house. Small secret rooms with disguised entrances—such as a door that looked like a bookcase—were also common. Some agents built sheds concealed within haystacks in nearby fields for the runaways' protection. At times, fugitives remained undetected in these sheds while determined slave catchers thoroughly searched the agent's house and barn.

Once the escaped slaves had rested and it was safe to leave, they were directed to the next Underground Railroad station. Sometimes they made the journey alone on foot, but when it was thought to be especially dangerous, Underground Railroad agents transported them

This house in Cincinnati, Ohio, was a stop on the Underground Railroad. The back porch of the house has a secret opening in the floor. Escaping slaves hid under the porch while waiting to move on to the next station.

in wagons. Frequently these wagons were built with false bottoms in which a person could hide. Abram Allen, an Underground Railroad agent from Oakland, Ohio, had a special wagon built that he called the Liberator. This oversized carrier could hold ten people, and its back was completely covered by a curtain.

Other times slaves riding in wagons hid under large piles of hay or straw. Some light-skinned runaways who could pass for white were dressed as farmers and given a buggy by the Underground Railroad agent so they could drive themselves to the next station.

Escape by Water

Though most runaways traveled by land, some took a water route to the North. This often proved to be a wise choice for slaves on plantations near the seacoast or in areas bordering rivers. In some cases, slaves stowed away on vessels, climbing aboard without the crew's knowledge and hiding somewhere on the ship. Other times, ship captains worked with the Underground Railroad, willingly hiding fugitives slaves on their vessels for free. Some runaway slaves were brought to Philadelphia by steamboat where the active vigilance committee there helped them get to Canada or find a safe place to settle in the North.

The Underground Railroad was especially active in the Great Lakes area. From there, thousands of fugitives were safely ferried to freedom in Canada. William Wells Brown was an escaped slave who found employment on a vessel that ran from Cleveland, Ohio, to Buffalo, New York, and Detroit, Michigan. Brown would often make an

A portrait of William Wells Brown, an escaped slave who was born in Kentucky. After his escape, he aided many other fugitives on their road to freedom.

important detour in these trips, as Underground Railroad agents discovered. Brown explained in his 1849 book *Narrative of William W. Brown, an American Slave*:

> It is well known that a great number of fugitives make their escape to Canada, by way of Cleaveland [Cleveland]; and while on the lakes, I always made arrangements to carry them on the boat to Buffalo, or Detroit, and thus effect [make possible] their escape to the "promised land." The friends of the slave [Underground Railroad workers], knowing that I would transport them without charge, never failed to have a delegation when the boat arrived at Cleaveland. I have sometimes had four or five aboard at one time.
>
> In the year 1842, I conveyed from the first of May to the first of December, sixty-nine fugitives over Lake Erie to Canada. In 1843 I visited Malden in upper Canada, and counted seventeen in that small village, whom I had assisted in reaching Canada.

Strength in Numbers

In places where most of the local people held strong abolitionist beliefs, friends and neighbors were often willing to help Underground Railroad agents protect fugitive slaves from slave catchers. That was the case when two slave catchers arrived in Attica, New York, to bring back a runaway slave named Statie and her young daughter.

The slave catchers' first stop was the town's post office, where they asked the postmaster if he knew where the two escaped slaves were. In his 1879 book *Sketches in the History of the Underground Railroad*, former Underground Railroad conductor Eber M. Pettit described what happened next:

> The Postmaster took them [the slave catchers] into his office and told them plainly that the slaves were within half a mile of the

*village, "but," he said, "you had better not try to take them. I
would be glad to help you if I dared to but every man, woman,
and child in the place would help them, and you can't raise men
enough in this county to take them away from here. I see by the
commotion in the streets that you are suspected already, and I
cannot answer for your safety if you should ever attempt to
prosecute [carry out] this business. Such a thing has never been
attempted here, and I tell you it will go hard with the man that
tries it. . . . I have nothing more to say on the subject, except that
I should think fifteen or twenty minutes is as long a time as it
will be safe for you to be seen in this town."*

*A glance at the crowd already gathered in the street was
sufficient to clinch the arguments of the Postmaster, so the slave
hunters mounted their horses and rode silently out of town, the*

LOOK OUT.—We understand that there are
severel slave hunters in the city looking for
some of God's creatures. We suppose the poor
slaves took it into their heads that they belong-
ed to themselves, if they think so, we have no
objections. It don't seem that these men are
content and happy. Oh! we forgot they gave
leg bail—this will do very well, as it iscus-
tomary to give security. Go it boys.

*This piece printed in an Ohio newspaper in 1844 warned of slave hunters in
the area.*

*people making no demonstration until they were on the bridge,
when a shout, a cheer, three times three, seemed to put new life
into their horses and they were soon out of sight.*

Looking back, I saw that my pursuers were gaining on me. They were not more than two hundred yards distant.
—Dr. Alexander Ross, an Underground Railroad conductor, 1855

RISKY BUSINESS

Escaping from slavery as well as helping others to do so was often a high-risk undertaking. Apprehended runaways frequently faced the harshest punishments as an example to others who might be tempted to do the same. Severe beatings, torture, and mutilation were common consequences for captured runaways. At times, slave owners used a branding iron to brand captured runaways with the letter *R* for "returned slave." Under the worst circumstances, the captured runaway might be murdered. One account of such a death appeared in the Ohio newspaper the *Castigator*:

> *We have it from undoubted authority that a slave was lately murdered in Henry County, Kentucky, in the following barbarous*

manner: The murderer had hired the slave [from his owner] and treated him with intolerable cruelty. Of course the slave ran away from him in order to gain a little respite from his sufferings. [The man he had been working for] pursued him, took him, and tied him to his horse and when extremely heated, drew him through a creek of cold running water. The consequence was that the unhappy creature soon became unable to keep on his feet, and when he fell to the ground, the unfeeling monster dismounted and beat him to death! The criminal was arrested; but the court of examination determined that it was a case of manslaughter and consequently bound him in a trifling sum to appear at the circuit court; and thus, he was let loose again. The most malicious, deliberate and barbarous murder of a slave is but man-slaughter!

Slave owners were especially anxious to punish individuals associated with the Underground Railroad. The owners felt certain that

Below: *Sometimes free African Americans were caught by slave hunters and forced into slavery.* **Facing page:** *Fugitive slaves stay a few steps ahead of slave catchers.*

without this widespread network, fugitive slaves would have a much harder time escaping their plantations and remaining undetected while on the run. At first, slave owners had relied on the Fugitive Slave Act from colonial times to protect their human property. This act made helping runaways a criminal offense. Anyone caught hiding an escaped slave might be fined five hundred dollars. Most people with the Underground Railroad were not wealthy. A fine that large would probably cause them to lose their farms or businesses.

Yet that didn't stop slaves from running away or those on the Underground Railroad from helping them. One well-known case from 1847 involved a shipowner named Captain Daniel Drayton. When he first became a captain, he knew that many slaves tried desperately to escape on ships headed north. But Drayton had little sympathy for them or for abolitionists. As Drayton, however, got to know more African Americans in the course of his work, his attitude changed. "I had found out," he noted in his memoirs, ". . . that they

Shipowner Daniel Drayton shipped escaping slaves north on his boat the Pearl.

had the same desires, wishes and hopes, as myself." So when an inter-
mediary boarded Drayton's ship, docked in Washington, D.C., with
the story of a slave woman, Drayton listened.

The woman, the mother of five children, was trying to rejoin her
husband, a free African American, in the North. Her master had
promised to let her buy her freedom by doing extra work for another
master to earn money. The woman had worked for a number of years
to meet her end of the bargain. But after she had paid for herself in
full, her owner went back on his word. He said that if she ever men-
tioned the matter again, he would sell her to a master in the Deep
South, where slaves were worked the hardest.

After hearing her story, Drayton took pity on the woman. He
allowed her and her children, along with a niece, to stow away on
his ship. That was Drayton's first trip bringing slaves out of the
South, but it would not be his last. Drayton and another captain
named Sayres were later convinced to transport seventy-six slaves
from Washington, D.C., on a ship called the *Pearl.*

This large-scale escape was to occur on the night of a big celebra-
tion in the city. The abolitionists hoped that people would be too
busy enjoying themselves to pay much attention to what their slaves
were doing. So after dark, the slaves quickly boarded the *Pearl,* and
the captains set sail.

At first, it seemed as though their escape would succeed. But the
captains had miscalculated the situation. The slave owners discovered
their servants and field hands were gone early the next morning, and
an alarm was raised.

When pressured, a slave who had driven some of the fugitives to
the wharf revealed the escape plan. The furious slave owners
demanded that law enforcement officials send out an armed steamer
to overtake the *Pearl.*

After being captured, Drayton, Sayres, and the escaped slaves were
brought back to Washington. They were met by an angry mob, some
of whom threatened the prisoners with knives. Fortunately, the police

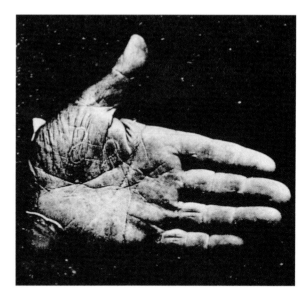

The Fugitive Slave Act made helping runaway slaves a crime. Captain Jonathan Walker had his hand branded with SS when he was caught assisting seven fugitive slaves. Antislavery advocates said that SS stood for "slave savior," while it stood for "slave stealer" in the South.

managed to get the prisoners to the jail safely. Drayton and Sayres were then bought to trial, facing forty-one criminal charges each. Drayton and Sayres was found guilty and both fined ten thousand dollars. Until they could pay their fines in total, they were to remain in prison.

Most of the African Americans who had tried to escape on the *Pearl* were returned to a life of slavery. Drayton and Sayres spent more than four years in prison before being pardoned by U.S. president Millard Fillmore.

Abolitionist Calvin Fairbanks was also punished severely for his abolitionist activities. Fairbanks, a Methodist minister, served as a conductor on the Underground Railroad, leading numerous slaves from throughout the South to freedom. Though he safely made many trips to the North with runaways, several times he was caught and whipped by slave owners.

Fairbanks also spent time in jail for his Underground Railroad activities. As he noted, "When called up for trial [for helping slaves escape] in February, . . . I pleaded guilty, and received a sentence of fifteen years. I served four years and eleven months, and then . . . was [pardoned] by Governor John J. Crittenden."

Despite what he'd been through, Fairbanks continued as an Underground Railroad conductor. As tensions between the North and South rose, however, the dangers rose for everyone involved with the Railroad. In 1850 the U.S. Congress passed a new Fugitive Slave Act—a harsher version of the colonial law.

Under the new act, the fine for aiding fugitive slaves was increased from five hundred to one thousand dollars. The law also extended the rights of slaveholders. The act provided that slaves could legally be returned to their owners even if those runaways had been living in the North as free men and women for years. As a result of the

An 1851 political cartoon depicts the controversy over the Fugitive Slave Act of 1850. On the left, abolitionist William Lloyd Garrison guards a slave woman against a slave catcher seated on the back of Daniel Webster. Webster, a U.S. senator, supported the harsh act.

These twenty men were arrested as they attempted to aid a fugitive slave. The Fugitive Slave Act of 1850 imposed even stricter sentences on people who tried to help those fleeing slavery. The Underground Railroad stayed strong despite the new law.

new law, some escaped slaves in the North resettled in Canada and England.

Yet if slaveholders had hoped to stall the Underground Railroad with the Fugitive Slave Act of 1850, it didn't work. Some scholars believe that the decade following the law's passage was the most active time for the Railroad. Fairbanks was among those who grew more determined than ever to see as many slaves as possible freed. While continuing his work, he was again arrested, just two years after being released from prison. This time Fairbanks was caught escorting a young slave woman to the North. He was tried and sentenced to fifteen years in prison.

While confined, he was treated brutally by prison guards because of his abolitionist views and actions. Over the years, he received more than thirty-five thousand lashes with a whip. After serving twelve years of his sentence, he was again pardoned and released.

Charles T. Torrey of Albany, New York, was another clergyman who served as an Underground Railroad conductor. Torrey was an abolitionist who believed that actions speak louder than words. He became extremely active in bringing slaves from the Washington, D.C., area to the northern states and Canada. His efforts freed a number of men, women, and children from bondage.

One of those freed was a young girl, five or six years old. As a slave, the girl was expected to stay awake through the night to serve her master and mistress. An African American Underground Railroad conductor named Thomas Smallwood who worked with Torrey described the little girl's situation:

> [The] child was required to set all night by the side of the cradle
> in its master's and mistress' bed chamber, in order that if their
> child should awake, she should rock [the baby], to prevent it
> from disturbing [her masters'] slumbers.

Torrey was eventually caught and arrested in Maryland trying to bring a slave family to freedom. He stood trial and was convicted. He was sentenced to eighteen years in prison—six years for each of the three slaves he was trying to help.

Numerous people signed the petitions sent to Maryland's governor and to the White House asking that Torrey be released. However, no pardon ever came. Torrey died alone in his prison cell.

The midnight sky and the silent stars have been the witnesses of your devotion to freedom and of your heroism.
—Frederick Douglass, in a letter to Harriet Tubman (left), 1868

TWO HEROES OF THE UNDERGROUND RAILROAD

Many individuals active in the Underground Railroad were required to make tremendous sacrifices. They lived with the constant threat of violence from slave owners who might decide to take the law into their own hands. At the same time, they often had to break the law themselves in service to their belief that they were obeying a higher law. Their frequently difficult position is obvious in the following letter sent from prison by an Underground Railroad conductor to his children:

My dear children, I want you to know that I am wholly innocent of all things for which I stand indicted. Give yourselves no concern about that. I am in irons [bonds and chains used on prisoners] for no fault. I have . . . [not] sinned against God. . . .

Your ever-loving Father

But even after making such sacrifices, not all Underground Railroad workers went down in history. Secrecy was crucial to the Railroad's operation, so countless instances of daring and bravery were never recorded in diaries, letters, or newspapers. Many heroes involved in the system remain nameless and faceless.

But some individuals made such exceptional contributions that they became well known. Among these was a white Quaker named Levi Coffin and an escaped African American slave named Harriet Tubman. Here are their stories.

Levi Coffin

Levi Coffin's distaste for slavery began when he was a young boy. Both his parents and grandparents were fiercely opposed to slavery and had never owned slaves. But growing up in North Carolina in the early 1800s, Coffin could not avoid the reality of the slave trade on a daily basis. Even at an early age, Levi Coffin felt frustrated at not being able to help when he saw slaves being abused. As he later wrote: "I was not always so fortunate as to be able to render assistance to the objects of my sympathy. I witnessed scenes of cruelty and injustice and had to stand passively by."

In one case, Coffin saw a slave owner come to pick up his captured slave. The slave left his master's plantation after the slave's wife was sold to a new owner. The slave had secretly followed the wagon carting his wife to her new plantation, hoping to see her one more time. However, he was caught along the way and returned to his master. His master was furious at the slave. Levi Coffin happened to be at the blacksmith's shop while the slave owner had the runaway put in irons for the trip home. Coffin recalled:

> *As I stood by and watched the scene . . . I longed to rescue the slave and punish the master. . . . I felt like fighting for the slave. . . . One end of the chain, riveted to the negro's neck, was made fast to the axle of his master's buggy, then the master sprang in and drove off at a sweeping trot, compelling the slave to run at full speed or fall and be dragged by his neck. I watched them till they disappeared in the distance, and as long as I could see them, the slave was running.*

The House at Newport

Levi Coffin never forgot the disturbing scenes he had witnessed in his youth. As an adult, he grew determined to do all he could to change things. In 1826 Levi Coffin and his wife, Catharine, moved to Newport, Indiana (present-day Fountain City). Levi Coffin became a successful merchant in his new town, but his most important work was for the Underground Railroad. In Newport the couple was able to put their abolitionist beliefs into action. For at least the next twenty years, they turned their simple eight-room house into an active safe haven for fugitive slaves heading north. Levi described what it was like:

> *In the winter of 1826–27, fugitives began to come to our house, and as it became more widely known on different routes [of the Underground Railroad] that the slaves fleeing from bondage would find a welcome and shelter at our house, and be forwarded safely on their journey, the number increased. Friends in the neighborhood, who had formerly stood aloof from the work, fearful of the penalty of law, were encouraged to engage in*

Levi Coffin's house in Indiana was a stop on the Underground Railroad. Coffin and his wife, Catharine, hid more than two thousand slaves over a twenty-year period.

it when they saw the fearless manner in which I acted, and the success that attended my efforts.

Coffin set an important example in his own community. He helped so many slaves that he became known as the president of the Underground Railroad. His home was frequently called Grand Central Station after the famously busy train depot in New York City. Escaped slaves felt safe at the Coffin residence and knew that they'd be admitted there at any hour of the night. "I would invite them, in a low tone," wrote Coffin, "to come in, and they would follow me into the darkened house without a word, for we knew not who might be watching and listening."

A portrait of Levi Coffin. Like many Quakers, Coffin felt morally obligated to be active in the cause of abolition.

One of Coffin's Stories

Among the fugitive slaves Levi Coffin helped was a slave woman named Eliza Harris. Harris nearly died fleeing from slavery with her baby. Her story so moved the antislavery novelist Harriet Beecher Stowe that she based the character of Eliza in her classic 1852 novel *Uncle Tom's Cabin* on Harris's actual experience. Levi Coffin remembered the real Eliza's plight this way:

> *Eliza Harris . . . a slave from Kentucky . . . found that she and her only child were to be separated. She had buried two children and was doubly attached to the one she had left. . . . When she found it was to be taken from her, she was filled with grief and dismay, and resolved to make her escape that night, if possible.*

Knowing that the Ohio River would be frozen solid at that time of year, Eliza hoped to walk across it. However, when she arrived at the

The title page from Uncle Tom's Cabin (left), *a book written about slavery in the United States by Harriet Beecher Stowe* (above) *in 1852*

riverbank, she found that the ice had broken up and was floating on the water in large chunks. After waiting another day for the ice to harden, Eliza learned that her pursuers were close by. Coffin details her ordeal:

> *With desperate courage she determined to cross the river, or perish in the attempt. Clasping her child in her arms she . . . ran toward the river, followed by her pursuers, who had just dismounted from their horses when they caught sight of her. [Eliza] . . . felt that she rather be drowned than to be captured and separated from her child. Clasping her babe to her bosom with her left arm, she sprang on to the first cake of ice, then from that to another and another. Some times the cake she was*

on would sink beneath her weight, then she would slide her child on to the next cake, pull herself up with her hands, and so continue her hazardous journey. She became wet to the waist with ice water, and her hands were benumbed with cold, but as she made her way from one cake of ice to another, she felt that surely the Lord was preserving and upholding her, and that nothing could harm her.

When she reached the Ohio side, near Ripley, she was completely exhausted and almost breathless. A man, who had been standing on the bank watching her progress with amazement and expecting every moment to see her go down, assisted her up the bank. After she had recovered her strength a little he directed her to a house on the hill, in the outskirts of town. She made her way to the place, and was kindly received and cared for. It was not considered safe for her to remain there during the night, so, after resting a while and being provided with food and dry clothing, she was conducted to a station on the Underground Railroad, a few miles farther from the river. The next night she was forwarded on from station to station to our house in Newport, where she arrived safely and remained several days.

Other fugitives arrived in the meantime, and Eliza and her child were sent with them, by the Greenville Branch of the Underground Railroad, to Sandusky, Ohio. They reached that place in safety and crossed the lake to Canada, locating finally at Chatham, Canada West.

Eliza and her child were just two of the fugitive slaves the Coffins helped. While Levi and Catharine lived in Indiana, about two thousand slaves passed through their home on their way to freedom. In 1847 the Coffins moved to Cincinnati, Ohio, where they continued to fight against slavery. They opened a store at which they refused to sell any goods made by slave labor.

Grateful Canadians

In the summer of 1854, Levi, Catharine, and their daughter went to Canada to attend a meeting. While there they toured the country and saw numerous people whom they had helped. Levi Coffin wrote about the trip:

> *Many other fugitives came and spoke to us, whom we did not recognize or remember until they related some incident that recalled them to mind. Such circumstances occurred in nearly every neighborhood we visited in Canada. Hundreds who had been sheltered under our roof and fed at our table, when fleeing from the land of whips and chains, introduced themselves to us and referred to the time, often fifteen or twenty years before, when we had aided them.*

Even after the Civil War ended slavery in the United States, Levi Coffin did what he could to help newly freed slaves. He gave money, clothing, food, and other necessary items to help them successfully begin a new life as a free people.

Harriet Tubman

If Levi Coffin was the best-known male agent on the Underground Railroad, Harriet Tubman was its most famous female conductor. Born a slave in Maryland's Dorchester County around 1820, Harriet Tubman's childhood was filled with hard work and severe beatings.

While Tubman was just a teen, she suffered a serious injury. Trying to protect another slave, she had stood between that slave and an angry overseer. The overseer picked up a heavy object and threw it at the man Tubman was trying to shield. It missed its mark and hit Tubman in the head instead. Though she survived, she never fully recovered. For the rest of her life, Tubman would experience spells in which she'd sleep for prolonged periods.

Escape

Confined to a life of slavery and beatings, Tubman dreamed of a peaceful freedom. She described that dream to her biographer, Sarah H. Bradford, in *Scenes in the Life of Harriet Tubman:*

> *And all that time, in my dreams and visions, I seemed to see a line, and on the other side of that line were green fields, and lovely flowers, and beautiful white ladies, who stretched out their arms to me over the line, but I couldn't reach them nohow. I always fell before I got to the line.*

Then, in 1849, when Tubman was about twenty or twenty-five, she decided to make a daring escape for that line. A rumor was circulating among the slaves that Tubman and two of her brothers were to be sent into the Deep South to work in the plantation fields. Tubman and her brothers decided it was time to make a break for the North and freedom.

At some point in the escape, however, Tubman's brothers became frightened. They turned back, leaving Tubman on her own. She watched them go and then started again on her journey. She hid by day and walked by night, following the North Star. After several days, she realized that she had crossed "the magic line, which then divided the land of bondage from the land of freedom."

Tubman was overjoyed to be free, but she knew she was alone in the North. Her thoughts turned back at once to everyone she had left behind. She decided then to return to the South to help others escape.

> *So it was with me. I had crossed the line. I was* free; *but there was no one to welcome me to the land of freedom. I was a stranger in a strange land; and my home, after all, was down in Maryland; because my father, my mother, my brothers, and sisters, and friends were there. But I was free, and* they *should*

be free. I would make a home in the North and bring them there, God helping me.

A Famous Underground Railroad Conductor

Over the next ten years, Tubman made nineteen trips back to the South to rescue other slaves. Reports suggest that she safely escorted more than three hundred slaves to the North on the Underground Railroad and never lost a single passenger.

In time, a myth grew up around Tubman. She became known as Moses, after the biblical character who led the Israelites out of Egypt, where they had been enslaved. It was said that whenever this small woman appeared on a plantation, men, women, and children

Harriet Tubman helped hundreds of slaves escape. By 1856 the reward for Tubman's capture rose to forty thousand dollars. Tubman armed herself with a rifle for her dangerous missions.

disappeared. Of course, there was some truth to the myth: Harriet led them to freedom.

Tubman piloted her escaped slaves to the North as she herself had escaped, traveling by night and hiding by day. Tubman and her charges climbed over mountains, forded rivers, and found their way through thick forests. They often had to lie hidden as their pursuers passed them. To keep the babies and children quiet, Tubman gave them paregoric, a drug to make them sleep.

Travel was difficult, and the fugitives often found themselves exhausted. Their feet bled, and their bones ached. Many were ready to give up, claiming that they could not travel any farther and wanted to go home. But Tubman feared that any fugitives who returned to their masters would be forced to confess details about the Underground Railroad. The dangers of letting anyone leave the group were too great, and Tubman sometimes used a gun to make her

Harriet Tubman (far left, with pan) *is pictured after the Civil War with some of the slaves she had led to freedom.*

point, telling exhausted escapees, "[Y]ou go on or die!" Tubman could not have led so many slaves to freedom if she had not been so tough and disciplined.

Though Tubman is best known for her work as an Underground Railroad conductor, she did still more for her people. Anxious to see slavery outlawed, Tubman became a sought-after speaker at antislavery meetings throughout the North. She also championed the cause of woman's rights. She argued that women needed to play a larger role in the abolitionist movement as well as in other areas of life.

During the Civil War between the North and the South, Tubman offered her services to the Union (Northern) army. She helped the Northern forces in a number of ways, and at different times, she served as a nurse, a spy, and a scout. Tubman was especially valuable to the North because of her knowledge of Southern terrain. As she had traveled so much as an Underground Railroad conductor, her knowledge of back roads and hidden trails proved crucial to the Union army as it penetrated the South.

Tubman repeatedly risked her life so that others could enjoy freedom. As abolitionist John Brown once said, Tubman was "one of the bravest persons on this continent."

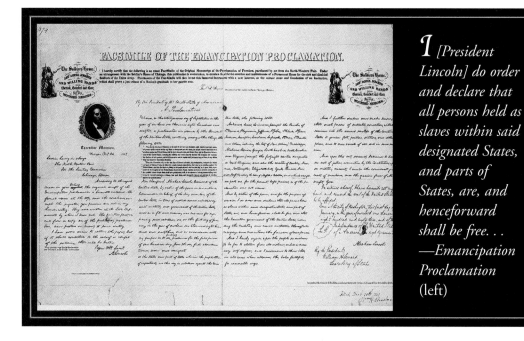

I [President Lincoln] do order and declare that all persons held as slaves within said designated States, and parts of States, are, and henceforward shall be free. . . .
—Emancipation Proclamation (left)

EPILOGUE

The network known as the Underground Railroad ended just as it had started—quietly. The need for it disappeared with the Civil War. With the North's victory in 1865, slavery ended. The brutal system that had kept African Americans in bondage for so long was crushed.

On January 1, 1863, at the height of the Civil War, President Abraham Lincoln had issued the Emancipation Proclamation freeing the slaves in areas under Southern control. After the Civil War, slavery was banned throughout the United States with the Thirteenth Amendment to the U.S. Constitution, passed into law on December 6, 1865. This simple but powerful law read:

Neither slavery or involuntary servitude, except as punishment for a crime whereof the party shall have been duly convicted, shall exist in the United States, or any place subject to their jurisdiction.

The Underground Railroad has a special place in our nation's history. In the most concrete way, it was literally the road to freedom. But was it actually much more than that?

Documenting the various paths used on the Underground Railroad can be daunting. The National Park Service found that out in a 1990 study on how best to interpret and commemorate the Railroad. After a special resource study, the park service determined that "the number of possible sites and structures associated with the Underground Railroad story is immense."

The Underground Railroad is every route that the enslaved took, or attempted to take to freedom. It is a vast network of paths and roads, through swamps and over mountains, along and across rivers and even by sea, that cannot be documented with precision.

The full social significance of the Railroad can be equally difficult to grasp. Partly, that is because it meant different things to different people. For enslaved African Americans, it was a way out of bondage. For many free African Americans, the Railroad represented a strong emotional and political commitment to the people they viewed as brothers and sisters.

For many white people, the Underground Railroad was a means of righting a serious wrong within American society. They firmly believed that slavery had no place in a democracy. Helping thousands of slaves to flee from their masters was a concrete way of calling attention to and working to right this injustice.

The Underground Railroad is also an outstanding example of how people of different races and backgrounds can successfully work together to achieve a common goal. Its historical example serves to remind any divided nation that none of us is truly free until all of us are free.

THE FUGITIVE SLAVE ACT OF 1850

As tensions over the issue of slavery grew in the years leading up to the Civil War, the U.S. government attempted to make some political compromises. The government wanted to appease both the antislavery advocates in the North and the pro-slavery forces in the South. In 1850, for example, California was admitted to the Union as a free state, and slave trading was outlawed in the District of Columbia. To balance these antislavery acts, the government revised the existing Fugitive Slave Act, expanding the rights of slave owners pursuing runaways.

For slaves, the Fugitive Slave Act of 1850 meant that courts and local police, even in the North, were required to help slave catchers. They were required to return fugitives to the states from which they had escaped, even if the fugitives had been living free for years. For Underground Railroad workers, the act meant that anyone found to have aided fugitive slaves could be thrown in jail and fined large amounts of money. Court systems and police forces were expanded to quickly put the new law into action.

Below are excerpts from the act. The sections detail the expansion of a force of commissioners, slave catchers with broad powers to pursue fugitives. These powers included being able to force ordinary citizens into a posse to hunt slaves. The sections also detail the penalties for police or citizens who refuse to enforce or obey the new law.

Section 3 And be it further enacted, That the Circuit Courts of the United States shall from time to time enlarge the number of the commissioners, with a view to afford reasonable facilities to reclaim fugitives from labor, and to the prompt discharge of the duties imposed by this act.

Section 4 And be it further enacted, That the commissioners above named shall have concurrent jurisdiction with the judges of the

Circuit and District Courts of the United States, in their respective circuits and districts within the several States, and the judges of the Superior Courts of the Territories, severally and collectively, in term-time and vacation; shall grant certificates to such claimants, upon satisfactory proof being made, with authority to take and remove such fugitives from service or labor, under the restrictions herein contained, to the State or Territory from which such persons may have escaped or fled.

Section 5 And be it further enacted, That it shall be the duty of all marshals and deputy marshals to obey and execute all warrants and precepts issued under the provisions of this act, when to them directed; and should any marshal or deputy marshal refuse to receive such warrant, or other process, when tendered, or to use all proper means diligently to execute the same, he shall, on conviction thereof, be fined in the sum of one thousand dollars, to the use of such claimant, on the motion of such claimant, by the Circuit or District Court for the district of such marshal; and after arrest of such fugitive, by such marshal or his deputy, or whilst at any time in his custody under the provisions of this act, should such fugitive escape, whether with or without the assent of such marshal or his deputy, such marshal shall be liable, on his official bond, to be prosecuted for the benefit of such claimant, for the full value of the service or labor of said fugitive in the State, Territory, or District whence he escaped: and the better to enable the said commissioners, when thus appointed, to execute their duties faithfully and efficiently, in conformity with the requirements of the Constitution of the United States and of this act, they are hereby authorized and empowered, within their counties respectively, to appoint, in writing under their hands, any one or more suitable persons, from time to time, to execute all such warrants and other process as may be issued by them in the lawful performance of their respective duties; with authority to such commissioners, or the persons to be appointed by them, to execute process as aforesaid, to summon and call to their aid the bystanders, or posse comitatus of the proper county, when necessary to ensure a faithful observance of the clause of the Constitution referred to, in conformity with the provisions of this act; and all good citizens are hereby commanded to aid and assist in the prompt and efficient execution of this law, whenever their services may be required, as aforesaid, for that purpose; and said warrants shall run, and be executed by said officers, any where in the State within which they are issued.

EMANCIPATION PROCLAMATION

On September 18, 1862, the Union army defeated Confederate forces at the Battle of Antietam in Maryland. It was an important victory for the North, and U.S. president Abraham Lincoln took the opportunity to issue a striking political declaration. On September 22, Lincoln signed the Emancipation Proclamation, declaring that as of January 1, 1863, slaves held in rebel states were free. It read, in part:

> I do order and declare that all persons held as slaves within said designated States, and parts of States, are, and henceforward shall be free; and that the Executive government of the United States, including the military and naval authorities thereof, will recognize and maintain the freedom of said persons.
>
> And I hereby enjoin upon the people so declared to be free to abstain from all violence, unless in necessary self-defence; and I recommend to them that, in all cases when allowed, they labor faithfully for reasonable wages.
>
> And I further declare and make known, that such persons of suitable condition, will be received into the armed service of the United States to garrison forts, positions, stations, and other places, and to man vessels of all sorts in said service.
>
> And upon this act, sincerely believed to be an act of justice, warranted by the Constitution, upon military necessity, I invoke the considerate judgment of mankind, and the gracious favor of Almighty God.

The proclamation was limited, as it only applied to states engaged in armed rebellion against the U.S. government. (Slavery remained in force in neutral border states.) But the proclamation still meant freedom for more than three million African American slaves. The proclamation also made slavery the central issue of the Civil War, convincing many freed slaves to join the Union army and fight to end the institution throughout the country.

Source Notes

A note on the sources: Every effort was made to use primary sources whenever possible. In many cases, nineteenth-century books have been reprinted exactly as is using modern paper and bindings. Available in many libraries and online, these reprints offer primary-source research that might otherwise be unavailable.

2 Maurice Duke, *Don't Carry Me Back! Narratives by Former Virginia Slaves* (Richmond: Dietz Press, 1995), 85.

6 Harriet Jacobs, *Incidents in the Life of a Slave Girl* (1861; repr. online at *Digital Schomburg African American Women Writers of the 19th Century*, http://digilib.nypl.org/dynaweb/digs/wwm97255/@Generic__BookView/, 1997), 16.

8 James L. Smith, *Autobiography of James L. Smith* (Norwich, CT: Bulletin Press, 1881), 33.

12 Kenneth M. Stampp, *The Peculiar Institution: Slavery in the Ante-Bellum South* (New York: Vintage Books, 1956), 141.

13 Norman R. Yetman, ed., *Voices from Slavery: 100 Authentic Slave Narratives* (Mineola, NY: Dover Publications, 1970), 135.

14 Kate E. R. Pickard, *The Kidnapped and the Ransomed. Being the Personal Recollections of Peter Still and His Wife "Vina," after Forty Years of Slavery* (New York: Miller, Orton and Mulligan, 1856), 28.

14–15 Ibid., 36.

15 John Hope Franklin and Alfred A. Moss Jr., *From Slavery to Freedom: A History of African Americans,* 7th ed. (1947; repr., New York: McGraw-Hill, 1994), 141.

17 Solomon Northup, *Twelve Years a Slave: Narrative of Solomon Northup* (Buffalo, NY: Derby, Orton and Mulligan, 1853), 166–168.

17 Ibid.

17 Peter Randolph, *Sketches of Slave Life: Or, Illustrations of the "Peculiar Institution"* (Boston: privately printed, 1855), 178.

17–18 Ibid., 179.

18 Duke, *Don't Carry Me Back!*, 88.

22 David Walker, quoted in "Africans in America: Judgment Day," *PBS Online,* 1999, http://www.pbs.org/wgbh/aia/part4/4p2930.html (August 8, 2005).

24–25 William Lloyd Garrison, *The Liberator,* inaugural editorial, January 1, 1831, quoted in "America's Civil War: Documents," *University of the South,* n.d., http://www.sewanee.edu/faculty/Willis/Civil_War/documents/Liberator.html (August 8, 2005).

26–27 William Wells Brown, "William Wells Brown Describes the Crafts' Escape, *The Liberator*, January 12, 1849," quoted in University of North Carolina at Chapel Hill, *Documenting the American South,* 2004, http://docsouth.unc.edu/neh/craft/support1.html (August 8, 2005).

27 David Walker, *Walker's Appeal* (1850; rev. ed. with an introduction by Sean Wilentz, New York: Hill and Wang, 1995), 85.

30 Charles L. Blockson, *The Underground Railroad: First Person Narratives of Escapes to Freedom in the North* (New York: Prentice Hall Press, 1987), 97.

32 Newspaper advertisement, *Macon (GA) Messenger,* May 25, 1837.

33–34 Henry Box Brown, *Narrative of the Life of Henry Box Brown, Written by Himself* (Manchester, UK: Lee and Glynn, 1851), ii–iii.

37–38 Wilbur H. Siebert, *The Underground Railroad from Slavery to Freedom* (New York: Macmillan Company, 1898), 65–66.

38–39 Ibid., 66.

39 Ibid.

40 Duke, *Don't Carry Me Back!,* 85.

41 Ann Hagedon, *Beyond the River: The Untold Story of the Heroes of the Underground Railroad* (New York: Simon & Schuster, 2002), 39.

43 Blockson, *The Underground Railroad,* 67.

43–44 Siebert, *The Underground Railroad from Slavery to Freedom,* 58.

47 William W. Brown, *Narrative of William W. Brown, an American Slave* (London: Charles Gilpin, 1849), 107.

47–49 Eber M. Pettit, *Sketches in the History of the Underground Railroad* (Fredonia, NY: W. McKinstry & Son, 1879), 79.

50 Alexander M. Ross, *Recollections and Experiences of an Abolitionist* (Toronto: Rowell and Hutchinson, 1875), 67–68.

50–51 Hagedorn, *Beyond the River,* 52.

52–53 Daniel Drayton, "Personal Memoir of Daniel Drayton," *Blackmask Online,* 2003, http://www.blackmask.com/thatway/books137c/memdradex.htm (June 20, 2005).

54–55 Siebert, *The Underground Railroad from Slavery to Freedom,* 159.

57 Blockson, *The Underground Railroad,* 155–56.

58 Sarah H. Bradford, *Scenes in the Life of Harriet Tubman* (Auburn, NY: W.J. Moses, 1869), 7.

59 Hagedon, *Beyond the River,* 133.

59 Levi Coffin, *Reminiscences of Levi Coffin* (Cincinnati: Robert Clarke Company, 1898), 20.

60 Ibid.

60–61 "Africans in America: Levi Coffin's Underground Railroad Station," *PBS Online,* 1999, http://www.pbs.org/wgbh/aia/part4/4h2946t.html (August 8, 2005).

61 "Indiana's Popular History: Levi Coffin," *Indiana Historical Society,* 2004, http://www.indianahistory.org/pop_hist/people/coffin.html (September 8, 2005).

62 Coffin, *Reminiscences,* 148.

63–64 Ibid., 149–150.

65 Ibid., 152.

66 Bradford, *Scenes in the Life of Harriet Tubman,* 16.

66 Sarah H. Bradford, *Harriet: The Moses of Her People* (New York: Geo. R. Lockwood & Son, 1886), 30.

66–67 Bradford, *Scenes in the Life of Harriet Tubman,* 20.

69 Bradford, *Harriet: The Moses of Her People,* 33.

69 "Africans in America: Judgment Day; Harriet Tubman," *PBS Online,* 1999, http://www.pbs.org/wgbh/aia/part4/4p1535.html (August 8, 2005).

70 "Emancipation Proclamation," *National Archive and Records Administration: Featured Documents,* n.d., http://www.archives.gov/exhibits/featured_documents/emancipation_proclamation/index.html (August 8, 2005).

70–71 Thirteenth Amendment to the U.S. Constitution, *The National Archives Experience: The Charters of Freedom,* n.d., http://www.archives.gov/national-archives-experience/charters/constitution_amendments_11-27.html (August 8, 2005).

71 National Park Service, *Taking the Train to Freedom: Underground Railroad Special Resource Study,* 1998, http://www.nps.gov/undergroundrr/ugsum.htm (June 20, 2005).

72–74 "Fugitive Slave Act of 1850," *Avalon Project at Yale Law School,* 1996, http://www.yale.edu/lawweb/avalon/fugitive.htm (August 8, 2005).

75 "Emancipation Proclamation," *National Archive and Records Administration: Featured Documents.*

Selected Bibliography

"Africans in America." *PBS Online.* N.d. http://www.pbs.org/wgbh/aia/home.html (September 8, 2005).

Blockson, Charles L. *The Underground Railroad: First Person Narratives of Escapes to Freedom in the North.* New York: Prentice Hall Press, 1987.

Bradford, Sarah H. *Harriet: The Moses of Her People.* New York: Geo. R. Lockwood & Son, 1886.

———. *Scenes in the Life of Harriet Tubman.* Auburn, NY: W. J. Moses, 1869. Also available online at University of North Carolina at Chapel Hill, *Documenting the American South,* 2004, http://docsouth.unc.edu/neh/bradford/bradford.html (September 8, 2005).

Brown, Henry Box. *Narrative of the Life of Henry Box Brown, Written by Himself.* Manchester, UK: Lee and Glynn, 1851.

Brown, William W. *Narrative of William W. Brown, an American Slave.* London: Charles Gilpin, 1849. Also available online at University of North Carolina at Chapel Hill, *Documenting the American South,* 2004, http://docsouth.unc.edu/brownw/menu.html (September 8, 2005).

Coffin, Levi. *Reminiscences of Levi Coffin.* Cincinnati: Robert Clarke Company, 1898.

Douglass, Frederick. *My Bondage and My Freedom.* New York: Washington Square Press, 1855.

Duke, Maurice. *Don't Carry Me Back! Narratives by Former Virginia Slaves.* Richmond: Dietz Press, 1995.

Franklin, John Hope, and Alfred A. Moss Jr. *From Slavery to Freedom: A History of African Americans.* 7th ed. 1947. Reprint, New York: McGraw-Hill, 1994.

Hagedon, Ann. *Beyond the River: The Untold Story of the Heroes of the Underground Railroad.* New York: Simon & Schuster, 2002.

"Indiana's Popular History: Levi Coffin." *Indiana Historical Society,* 2004. http://www.indianahistory.org/pop_hist/people/coffin.html (September 8, 2005).

National Park Service. *Taking the Train to Freedom: The Underground Railroad Special Resource Study.* 1998. http://www.nps.gov/undergroundrr/ugsum.htm (September 8, 2005).

Northup, Solomon. *Twelve Years a Slave: Narrative of Solomon Northup.* Buffalo: Derby, Orton and Mulligan, 1853. Also available online at University of North Carolina at Chapel Hill, *Documenting the American South,* 2004, http://docsouth.unc.edu/northup/northup.html (September 8, 2005).

Pettit, Eber M. *Sketches in the History of the Underground Railroad.* Fredonia, NY: W. McKinstry & Son, 1879.

Pickard, Kate E. R. *The Kidnapped and the Ransomed. Being the Personal Recollections of Peter Still and His Wife "Vina" after Forty Years of Slavery.* New York: Miller, Orton and Mulligan, 1856. Also available online at Indiana University (Bloomington), *Wright American Fiction 1851–1875.* 2002. http://www.letrs.indiana.edu/cgi/t/text/text-idx?c=wright2;idno=wright2-1893 (September 8, 2005).

Quarles, Benjamin. *Black Abolitionists.* New York: Oxford University Press, 1969.

Randolph, Peter. *Sketches of Slave Life: Or, Illustrations of the "Peculiar Institution."* Boston: privately printed, 1855. Also available online at University of North Carolina at Chapel Hill, *Documenting the American South.* 2004. http://docsouth.unc.edu/neh/randol55/randol55.html (September 8, 2005).

Ross, Alexander M. *Recollections and Experiences of an Abolitionist.* Toronto: Rowell and Hutchinson, 1875.

Siebert, Wilbur H. *The Underground Railroad from Slavery to Freedom.* New York: Macmillan Company, 1898.

Smith, James L. *Autobiography of James L. Smith.* Norwich, CT: Bulletin Press, 1881.

Stampp, Kenneth M. *The Peculiar Institution: Slavery in the Ante-Bellum South.* New York: Vintage Books, 1956.

Switala, William J. *Underground Railroad in Pennsylvania.* Mechanicsburg, PA: Stackpole Books, 2001.

Yetman, Norman R., ed. *Voices from Slavery: 100 Authentic Slave Narratives.* Mineola, NY: Dover Publications, 1970.

Further Reading and Websites

Books

Arnold, James R. *The Civil War.* Minneapolis: Lerner Publications Company, 2005. Civil War scholar Arnold chronicles the conflict that ended slavery in the United States.

Arnold, James R., and Roberta Wiener. *Divided in Two: The Road to the Civil War.* Minneapolis: Lerner Publications Company, 2002. This book details the growing rift between life in the North and in the South as the debate over slavery intensified in the years before the Civil War.

Currie, Stephen. *The Liberator: Voice of the Abolitionist Movement.* San Diego: Lucent Books, 2000. Currie looks at the history of William Garrison's abolitionist newspaper and describes its role in the anti-slavery movement.

Ferris, Jeri. *Go Free or Die: A Story about Harriet Tubman.* Minneapolis: Carolrhoda Books, Inc., 1988. This books profiles one of the most famous workers on the Underground Railroad, from her life as a slave to her career as a fearless conductor.

Fradin, Dennis Brindell. *Bound for the North Star: True Stories of Fugitive Slaves.* New York: Clarion, 2000. Fradin uses historical accounts and primary sources to detail twelve stories of escaped slaves.

Gorrell, Gena K. *North Star to Freedom: The Story of the Underground Railroad.* New York: Delacorte Press, 1997. Gorrell focuses on the Underground Railroad in Canada, including the work of Canadian Quakers and abolitionists.

Hamilton, Virginia. *Many Thousand Gone: African Americans from Slavery to Freedom.* New York: Knopf, 1993. Original art highlights this account of African Americans from colonial times through the Civil War.

Hansen, Joyce, and Gary McGowan. *Freedom Roads: Searching for the Underground Railroad.* Chicago: Cricket Books, 2003. This book looks at the known paths slaves took to freedom, while discussing the many types and limits of historical evidence about the Underground Railroad.

Haskins, James, and Kathleen Benson. *Following Freedom's Star: The Story of the Underground Railroad.* New York: Benchmark Books, 2002. This book examines the workings of the Underground Railroad by looking at the stories of escaped slaves, a fugitive living in the North, and a conductor.

Kallen, Stuart A. *Life on the Underground Railroad.* San Diego: Lucent, 2000. Kallen looks at life under slavery and the desperate risks taken by runaways.

Kenschaft, Lori J. *Lydia Maria Child: The Quest for Racial Justice.* New York: Oxford University Press, 2002. This book profiles Child, a successful author of her time who became a vocal abolitionist.

Landau, Elaine. *Slave Narratives: The Journey to Freedom.* Danbury, CT: Franklin Watts, 2001. The individual stories of several slaves are used to paint a picture of life on a plantation.

Lilley, Stephen R. *Fighters against American Slavery.* San Diego: Lucent Books, 1999. Lilley details the work of six key abolitionists: Benjamin Lundy, William Lloyd Garrison, Frederick Douglass, Harriet Tubman, Nat Turner, and John Brown.

Websites

Library of Congress. *Born in Slavery: Slave Narratives from the Federal Writers' Project, 1936–1938.*
http:// www.memory.loc.gov/ammem/snhtml/snhome.html
In the 1930s, the Federal Writers' Project, a U.S. government undertaking, conducted twenty-three hundred interviews with African Americans who had been slaves. The stories and accompanying

photographs were microfilmed in 1941 and added to the Library of Congress's website in 2001. Visitors to the site can read the former slaves' own words and view hundreds of photographs, some never before available to the public.

———. *Resource Guide for the Study of Black History & Culture.* "The African-American Mosaic."
http://www.loc.gov/exhibits/african/intro.html
The Library of Congress's resource for African American history features a section on abolition. Historical publications and illustrations detail the growth of the abolitionist movement and its conflict with pro-slavery forces.

National Underground Railroad Freedom Center.
http://www.undergroundrailroad.org
Explore the people and places associated with the Underground Railroad on this website, and see what lessons on freedom the Railroad holds for us today.

National Underground Railroad Network to Freedom.
http://www.cr.nps.gov/ugrr
Learn about the places where the Underground Railroad was most active. Don't miss the featured stories on this website.

Places to Visit

Frederick Douglass National Historic Site
Washington, D.C.
(202) 426-5961
http://www.nps.gov/frdo/
Visitors to abolitionist publisher Douglass's onetime home will learn about his personal and political achievements.

Harriet Beecher Stowe Center
Hartford, Connecticut
(860) 522-9258
http://www.harrietbeecherstowecenter.org/
Abolitionist writer Stowe's home and library house a large collection of diaries, manuscripts, photographs, and historic posters.

Harriet Tubman House
Auburn, New York
(315) 252-2081
http://www.nyhistory.com/harriettubman/
The site of Underground Railroad conductor Tubman's former home houses a library and an assembly hall. Tours are available year-round.

Levi Coffin House State Historic Site
Fountain City, Indiana
(765) 847-2432
http://www.state.in.us/ism/HistoricSites/LeviCoffin/Historic.asp
Visitors can tour the house where Levi and Catharine Coffin hid more than two thousand slaves over twenty years as agents on the Underground Railroad.

National Underground Railroad Freedom Center

Cincinnati, Ohio

(877) 648-4838

http://www.freedomcenter.org

Opened in 2004, the Freedom Center uses artifacts, exhibits, and interactive displays to evoke the experience of African American slavery and escape. Visitors can even climb into a replica of the box Henry Brown used to mail himself to freedom.

Ripley, Ohio

http://www.ripleyohio.net/

This small town in southwestern Ohio was a center of activity for the Underground Railroad. Just across the Ohio River from the slave state of Kentucky, Ripley became a transit point for thousands of fugitive slaves. The town features two national historic landmarks, the John Rankin House and the John Parker House. Rankin, a white Prebysterian minister, and Parker, an African American inventor and business owner, were two of Ohio's most famous Railroad conductors. Both houses offer educational tours.

Second Baptist Church

Detroit, Michigan

(313) 961-0920

Detroit's Second Baptist Church is the oldest African American Baptist church in the Midwest. From 1836 to 1865, the church was a station on the Underground Railroad. About five thousand slaves took refuge there before traveling across the Detroit River to Canada. Still an active parish, the church complex includes a museum, a bookstore, and a reconstructed hideout. Tours are available by appointment.

Index

Acknowledgments

The images in this book are used with the permission of: © Bettmann/CORBIS, p. 6; Library of Congress, pp. 8 (LC-USZ62-76081), 16 (LC-B811- 211), 19 (LC-USZ62-111153), 23 (LC-USZ62-40758), 25, 28, 34 (LC-USZ62-1283), 50 (LC-USZ62-30803), 51 (LC-USZ62-200596), 52, 55 (LC-USZ62-28755), 58 (LC-USZ62-7816), 63 (right), 67, 70 (LC-USZ62-98513); Independent Picture Service, pp. 9, 10; Documenting the American South (http://docsouth .unc.edu), The University of North Carolina at Chapel Hill Libraries, pp. 11 (from *Narrative of the Life and Times of Frederick Douglass, an American Slave, Written by Himself,* Boston, 1845), 22 (from *Walker's Appeal in Four Articles: Together with a Preamble, to the Coloured Citizens of the World, but in Particular, and Very Expressly, to Those of the United States of America, Written in Boston, State of Massachusetts, September 28, 1829,* Boston, 1830), The Library of Virginia, p. 12; National Archives (NWDNS-111-BA-1103), p. 15; map by Laura Westlund, p. 20; Ohio Historical Society, pp. 26, 32, 41, 45, 46, 48, 56; Madison County Historical Society, Oneida, New York, p. 30; C. T. Webber, *The Underground Railway,* Cincinnati Art Museum, p. 36; J. Y. Joyner Library Special Archives, East Carolina University, from *Narrative of the Life and Adventures of Henry Bibb, An American Slave, Written by Himself,* New York, 1849, p. 37; Eastman Johnson, *A Ride for Liberty–The Fugitive Slaves,* courtesy, Brooklyn Museum of Art, p. 40; © North Wind Picture Archive, p. 42; The Massachusetts Historical Society, p. 54; Indiana Historical Society, pp. 61 (P0391), 62 (C8819); Special Collections, Ellis Library, University of Missouri Colombia, p. 63 (left); © Sophia Smith Collection/Smith College, p. 68.

Front cover: Smithsonian American Art Museum, Washington, D.C./ Art Resource, NY.

Titles from the award-winning People's History Series:

Accept No Substitutes! The History of American Advertising

Declaring Independence: Life During the American Revolution

Don't Whistle in School: The History of America's Public Schools

Dressed for the Occasion: What Americans Wore 1620–1970

Failure Is Impossible! The History of American Women's Rights

The Fight for Peace: A History of Antiwar Movements in America

Good Women of a Well-Blessed Land: Women's Lives in Colonial America

Headin' for Better Times: The Arts of the Great Depression

Into the Land of Freedom: African Americans in Reconstruction

Journalists at Risk: Reporting America's Wars

Thar She Blows: American Whaling in the Nineteenth Century

This Land Is Your Land: The American Conservation Movement

Uncle Sam Wants You! Military Men and Women of World War II

We Shall Overcome: The History of The American Civil Rights Movement

What's Cooking? The History of American Food

For more information, please call 1-800-328-4929 or visit www.lernerbooks.com